Also by Alexandria Peary

POETRY

Fall Foliage Called Bathers & Dancers

Lid to the Shadow

Control Bird Alt Delete

The Water Draft

COVID Spring: Granite State Pandemic Poems (editor)

COVID Spring II: More Granite State Pandemic Poems (editor)

NONFICTION

Prolific Moment: Theory and Practice of Mindfulness for Writing

Creative Writing Pedagogies for the Twenty-First Century
(with Tom C. Hunley)

Battle of Silicon Valley at Daybreak

Alexandria Peary

Spuyten Duyvil
New York City

Acknowledgements

Many thanks to the editors in whose magazines these poems appeared: Action, Spectacle; American Poetry Journal; Barrow Street; Boston Review; Broadkill Review; Green Mountains Review; Hotel Amerika; Interim; Lotus-eater; Main Street Rag; New American Writing; North American Review; Northern New England Review; Pangyrus; Plume; Shearsman Magazine; Sixth Finch; web Conjunctions; Yale Review; and Yew. The author is grateful to the Academy of American Poets for a 2020 Poets Laureate Fellowship and for Salem State University for their support of her creative work.

ISBN 978-1-956005-36-3
Cover art: "The Battle of Silicon Valley" by Jennifer (Shon) Hill jennifercshill.com

Library of Congress Cataloging-in-Publication Data

Names: Peary, Alexandria, 1970- author.
Title: Battle of Silicon Valley at daybreak / Alexandria Peary.
Description: New York City : Spuyten Duyvil, [2022] |
Identifiers: LCCN 2021048642 | ISBN 9781956005363 (paperback)
Subjects: LCGFT: Poetry.
Classification: LCC PS3616.E266 B38 2022 | DDC 811/.6--dc23
LC record available at https://lccn.loc.gov/2021048642

Dedicated to my father,
Richard Linwood Peary

Contents

Preface

In the preface, a book blurb floats with the author bio along an upside-down menu as a mid-sized paragraph swims into view and bumper-cars a stanza. It's a microcosm of structures and genres! We glimpse the large barge of a paragraph slipping around the lower right-hand corner of the page—it was loaded with recycled language, compressed to reduce volume, slightly corroded. What was the paragraph about? It didn't seem to concern itself with poetry or poetics. Take a screenshot of the preface: a Netflix show plays Jacks with a sonnet, a status update from social media chitchats with a couplet. Ah, you say, this collection, you turn to inspect the back cover, then open the inside flap, appears to lack a blurb or testimonies by reviewers. The blurbs have been whited-out to match the Ikea bookshelves. On top of that, we notice the writing process, normally kept in a cubby in the proverbial roll top desk of writerly isolation… freewriting in gold script, ghost sheets of prewriting, a flotilla of editing. Modes and moments. Pointing these parts out, drawing them out, might make visible other power structures and limitations. With genre-inside-a-genre (business templates, YA novel, recipes, disclaimers, a wedding announcement, an immigration policy, a social studies textbook), more audiences are pulled into the room of a poem—and more contexts, so more rooms-in-rooms. Here comes a footnote, no longer a bottom feeder, and a flashback releases the syllables of three air bubbles. Why not let genres live a life as detail? Steel and hand-hewn beams lean on the back of the preface and take a well-deserved break from the structures (poetic, socio-economic, racial, gendered) they normally uphold. How does the immense bulk of writing stay upright? No problem. Hey, the bio mutated in the last thirty seconds: *At our convenience store at Our Lady of Genre at Frank D'Angelo's Café on the frontispiece of the gas station near the chapters of Peary's Market near the subtitle in the table of contents, deliveries were opened on Tuesdays with a box cutter—paragraph boxes. To earn those agnostic gumballs, Swedish fish, sour parody, atomic fireballs of appropriation, simulated cow tails, intertextual jawbreakers, we three kids killed flies for a penny, 56 blood-winged per Styrofoam cup.* In five hours and fifty-six minutes, this preface will wake up inside one of the genres it mentions—the container becomes contents (or content), and vice versa: the Pantheon is sitting inside a shoe closet, waiting for a vaccination appointment.

POEM WITH FRUIT FLIES

Fruit flies in the ballpoint bowl are attracted to
the voice in the blue ink of script pears, the Calibri nectarines in
a bowl set at the start of a sentence, at the end, or within
easy reach in the middle, on a doily. In the depicted space, in
the wings, fruit flies collectively swing outside the margin on
the left, then the right, like a flock of commas in
a tight pack, as the poem itself floats to
the top of the page, rotates counterclockwise like a face on
a pillow, gives us a sideways look, beheaded ghost warrior monk in
several spots on the screen, in reverse, upside down,
a little whorl of phrases, like a red wax stamp, in
the signature style, "an iconography by which
she could be immediately recognizable," a still-life fingerprint.

The Storycomb

Fruit flies land on the poem & change the poem,
downloading content. Fruit flies are flecks of being & energy,
shifting the piece closer to prewriting & propelling
        it hours ahead, to editing, sending it back,
the poem resting on a simple table near the open window of a line break.
Because of drowsy proofreading moths & spellcheck wasps
fruit flies add voice to metallic fruit, softening the font. Fruit flies
add their two syllables, the voiceless sound of labiodental fricative,
meaning the vocal cords do not vibrate, unlike honey bees with pompom socks
        like pocket-sized yellow dual language dictionaries:
German bees, the Italian honey bee *Apis mellifera liquistica,* & Russian bees
—though it's a narrative bee who lures us into the storycomb,
phrase by phrase a maze, so a mascot hornet emerges
        from the margin, bootlegs a sweet peachy part, a noun with hooks,
causing fruit flies to land again on the poem & change the poem.

Oysters and Fruit

Between quotation marks the eating is good.
It's "   " and ""between quotation marks""
and 'quotation marks' in a heap with italic shadows.
        Digging deeper into the pile, "bivalves…"
"frond-lipped, brine stung," shucked and syllabic
near "the tang" of "pure verb"
as *I thought hard for us all—my only swerving—*

Eleven black syllables recline on the silver platter
of the beginning, in bunches of letters, near
hourglass & swoosh shapes. It becomes rubble
in the mouth, a mill torn down.
        Demolition begins w/ spinning room,
tanning facility, turrets on the locker room,
then the browse line, clouds in quote marks.
Line by line, the poem rolls up as a sushi mat, snaps
like a plastic window shade.

1. Shake a packet of directions.[1]
2. Spit out the seeds of surprise to indicate
motion outside a pear.
3. Use the superscript spoon provided
to remove four paper tabs
and dig at concave or convex meaning
lightly salted with rental rooms.
If they sell soft serve, it's self-serve.
Behind the Stonehenge of your teeth,
the wave of the tongue waits
to scatter agnostic gumballs.

---

1 Frank D'Angelo, "The Rhetoric of Intertextuality," *Rhetoric Review*, Volume 29, Issue 1, 2009: adaptation, retro/recycling, appropriation, parody, pastiche, simulation. Good Eats.

Paraphrased First Supper

•

Still life in the middle of a sentence, still life at the end of a sentence, still life at the beginning. Every time we tried to pass an item—the bread basket, a fork of recommendation, the ghost of red wine—over the plank table, a still life blocked our attempt.

•

Wherever our white glove went, operated by the eye, the still life moved. It leapt to the middle of the sentence, to the start, to the end, across a plot ironed into table linens, a feast shared by *friends and not servants.* It was simultaneously a first discourse and farewell discourse. It leapt cat-like, the Snow Cat, the snow leopard that moved like machinery, bristled, blocking us this way, then that way.

•

"To love one another as I have loved you" was how the toast went. We had rented event space at the Lions Club, not the Rotary, for the tiled vanishing point in the renaissance perspective behind the banquet table. As the polar cat rubbed our ankles in secret under the table, we listened to the discourse of farewell on the first page of the first book, all twelve of us, collected like poems.

•

One of us was thinking, "Maybe it's easy to be loved by friends when the stakes are so high," after knocking over the salt cellar. He is the scowling figure with the loosened tie. Then the more outgoing of us, the thrower of our perpetual bachelor parties, declared to every folding chair, "In the bronze words of the founder Melvin Jones, 'You can't get very far until you start doing something for somebody else.'"

•

A basket of fruit blocked the end of the world, the beginning of the world, a still life like a planet, an earthy anecdote before an invective against swans. We picked up our appetizer spoons and ate the inside of parenthesis. We used the wrong spoon, the demitasse instead of the bouillon. When we finally ate anything, it was rough and tangy happy loss, wild parsnips from a lawn of scallions.

Analysis of A Poem on the Tablecloth

I.e.: Cezanne apples, Botero oranges, Roy Lichtenstein grapes,
Williams plums, a Gertrude Stein carafe in a poem on the tablecloth.
Re: A bowl of poems, color modulated melody
and objects avoiding personification,
the dish celestial blue and the oranges obese,
the plums lecherous and the apples suffering vertigo
b/c of the tablecloth, the slopes of the fabric
like a terrain windblown, rocky, with a survey of clouds,
lavender growing at the base, a tablecloth made from freewriting.
C/o fruit drawn in with a Bic ballpoint, fruit mentioned near a Mont Blanc
punctuated by clouds: % lemon and pewter ampersand, commas
on either side of the cobalt water pitcher,
blind copied and in the subject line
& all the other writing that exists alongside, between, near,
before, after, above, under, inside, around a finished poem,
those white bands of sentences, but also a strip from a user's agreement,
another from a romance novel, shiny, recycled, metallic, patterned, dented:
aluminum sentences or lines with edges curling upward
from a grant application, a wedding announcement, a monograph on immigration policy.

I ♥ My Cat Still Life

Heaped on a cut-crystal sentence
of average length, with two or three clauses,
one independent & the rest dependent,
the square fruit is in automatic or blue accent 2,
with a repeated line from a disclaimer
making window blinds (lowered) to prevent a migraine.

What Kenneth Goldsmith said is *our screen world*
is merely a thin skin under which resides miles and miles
of language, line command descriptions of systems
unfurling, fonts loading, and graphic packages
decompressing, and the html> under the floor

        is like a sink hole beneath the basement
                as I retype in brite January lite Wallace Stevens'
        "Sunday Morning" on my Dell laptop. Coffee
        & oranges in a sunny chair: I reach for a bluish apple
        and take a bite when a mewing comes
                from the Persian rug covering the DOS startup text.

It's kittens on the job, kittens w/ quarterbacks,
kittens on the naked shoulders of firemen & police,
kittens w/ priests! An adorable blue-eyed Siamese
poses close to basic sentences like in an early reader.
Script kitty plays w/ dust bunny. See script kitty run!

                        What? So that kitten is clickbait?!?
Throwing glances over its shoulder like grenades,
pretty kitty runs straight to the door of the dark web
hidden behind a designer pillow on the wing-back chair
guarded by a dozen dust bunnies carrying AK47.

Actual kittens held for ransom by an army of bots.

You have 4 hours to locate the nearest bitcoin
ATM. YOUR TIME STARTS NOW.
Okay, okay, mister booming movie trailer voice:
None of this is what I had in mind when I typed "coffee & oranges"
though it's because I typed "coffee & oranges" that I'm
running into a labyrinth of illicit desire & trade,

thru the Dream Market for murder/mayhem as vender
editors shout kill rates, past the cliff cave system
with holes marked Elections & Cyber Marriages.
Who would've guessed that a 20th-century American poet stands
above such darkness, such places of consequence?

With seconds to spare, I avoid Biblical punishments, *e.g.*:
- a wreath of bees will exit from my mouth,
- my nephew's dorm room will catch on fire,
- a flash flood will claim my baby grand piano.

What about Robert Hayden? Ashbery? Jane Miller? Jorie Graham?

Enter here carrying the last four digits, your mother's maiden,
employee identification, evil eye, crucifix, carved man,
your belief in democracy, your hail mary, security question,
return policy, your order #, your code. Push aside
that boulder of disclaimer.

Not the Raft of the Medusa

I spend days crossing on this raft of phrases:
hours as opaque as the room in the back of paintings
in which the narrative glow is up front,
my hand dipping into boxes of water, time in boxes,
not afraid of white sharks, an idea of sharks secondhand,
not anatomically correct, modeled on incandescent taxidermy.

I watch for the seams below in Alain Robbe-Grillet
in the labyrinth, Gorgio Chirico's *Hebdormous,*
-to catch when the gray subject changes-
-like watching a fountain of the present, cascade of moments-
On a raft of changes, I move above zig-zag water
colored in like a Missoni with ambition, curiosity, fear,

determination, irritation, hope, with vintage pastels
of Cuban cars, of buildings in Prague, colored in French,
German, English, Italian near where the Spanish Steps
stagger into hypnotic water a man with muscular shoulders
is banishing his daughters and wrestling a toothy fish
in the shop a beautiful dress is like a window covered in lemons

girls, that dress would cost us ten paychecks the pickpocket
flattens his hand into a spatula in that tourist's pocket
between open shutters Calvino's typing swings in a bird cage.

Counterfeit Clarice Last Lispector

•

We turn the floodlights on the actors, extras in one of the world's great short stories, surprising them mid-escapade, nocturnal animals caught playing dress up with our clothing, our fanciest possessions. Pearl choker on a possum, suit jacket on a raccoon. A skunk, a lynx, two tubby foxes moonlighting as twin nephews or as young men dating our daughters. How is it that standing beside a skunk in a man's shirt vest, holding a buggy bouquet of Queen Anne's lace to her throat, the possum manages to look haughty, even with those beady red eyes? *Hey*, that's my mother's apple seed necklace and that's her charm bracelet with a silver hula dancer with swaying hips, and, Elizabeth, that's your mother's last watch!

•

Garage floodlights ablaze, twelve apostles dine on a long table that appears to be a closet door supported by sawhorses in a formal space, like a rented banquet hall at the VFW. Caught red handed in the act of pretending they are us, in costume, at a picnic table of a table, in a Biblical scene set in Brazil. Startled, they hold poses, but insolently! Those eyes on the possum glint like rubies, and no one has a kind thought toward another. All turn inward, spiteful, sarcastic, jealous, resentful. Though one of us, maybe me, maybe you, maybe the neighbor with trash spewed along his driveway, is prepared to forgive.

•

They hold those poses until the wine not really wine is served & the beautiful fruits and vegetables are examples of providence, served with allegorical dessert, the undeserved kindness & generosity of a needlepoint of wheat sheaves. With phrases like *pineapples malignant in their savagery, calm and orangey oranges,* the fish stretched out and watchful like a silvery saint and those masochistic grapes! Most of all, it's about the bread in this story, those loaves and scones and crumpets, those rolls of transfiguration. A goblet tips over, crumbs race across the table cloth, melted wax leads to a still life already spoiling in this climate, all the choices we made are rusting. Because how long since we left our seat at the table?

"The Fish," on a Plate

The fish, all forty lines
like feathery bones fanned out
on a plate of unpolished silver, a shield or hubcap
displayed by Coptic Peter tableside.
[C]row-blue mussel shells
bespattered jelly fish, crabs like green / lilies
is served with timber by Marsden Hartley,
a crisscross of fallen men, medals
and ribbons along with Marsden Hartley's Heart,
decorated, —parsley of elms.

All forty lines of the Fish
an ichthys formed by Greek letters,
a secret sign, sprinkled with salt
from Sand Hill back home in Augusta,
ME, poured from a cathedral amid triple-deckers,
a Neruda tomato and Greek poet coffee,
overturned cup, a mess of lemons.
[C]hasm-side, the one who will always get away,
American shad, eel, Alewife
Blueback herring, Rainbow smelt
Tomcod, sea lamprey, the sign of the fish
near licenses plates—3 o'clock traffic.

Western Civ 101

The ant tracks of time   look like footbridges
made of hyphens   (3 or 4 hyphens per bridge)
black and white rainbows   archways above
phrases like diacritics   over bottles and jars
(these items out of focus, soft focus, just nouns)
—similar to a breve ŏ or an inverted breve ȏ,
a Latin small letter with circumflex, or a macron with grave ṑ.

The ant tracks of time   appear near a thesis statement,
above a wall of description   a corridor of narration
near a subtitle   over the door frame to an example:
college students taking a summer course read an essay
on noise and distraction by Seneca
                              when a bridge of hyphens
appears on the third line. It's followed by a bridge
over the second phrase in the twenty sixth, *I cannot*
for the life of me coming long after *I have lodgings right over*
a public bathhouse, which is separated by months
from *see that quiet is as necessary to a person*
as it is usually thought to be, the order different in time,
sequence of writing, sequence of reading,
as a jackhammer pounds and a crane lifts steel rafters
into a skyscraper, a new dorm under construction,
a giant statue of a tyrant is erected by a 100 slaves
in the crowded streets of Rome. Dust on sandals.
                                        During bridge repair,

the ants cross
a plank over
the construction site
to a small hole
in the stanza

of a vacant lot
leading to an underground crossword puzzle
of tunnels & dens,   razed & redacted rooms,
repressed & collective corridors   an alternative textbook,
an anthology of excerpts   adding to their stash:
i) the image of a head fallen from a statue
ii) the axle of a torched motive
iii) a cornice of a stone statement
and are supervised by the white ant that patrols
the rows, Control Alt Delete—
                                        warrior ants, explorer ants,
diplomat ants, teaching assistant ants, sales representative
ants, dietician ants, second cousin ants, pastor ants, actor ants,
architect ants, seamstress and tailor ants, high school sweetheart ants,
mercenary ant, beautician ants, translator ant, editor ants,
shoe store clerk ants, a fat June bug, street cleaner ant,
a bee on its back, waiter ants, mandibles of predatory lending,
police tape between pinchers. Fun fact:

Seneca was the tutor of Nero who requested his suicide
& Seneca submitted his resignation in a bathtub,
not as bad as suffocating minor enemies in rose petals?

Puzzle 26

in an underground crossword puzzle of tunnels & dens
vault   storehouse   cave
                                        banks   cellar   self-storage units
connected by tiny ladders
                                                3 down, 2 across
worker ants in hardhats
push *x* and *y* closer   making a Mad Lib

from the rubble of enigma with relics of nostalgia
a Doric detail   Times New Roman image
                                a few painted verbs   stolen items
or rentals never returned
                                                (that U-Haul)
in razed & redacted rooms
of erasure poems   & classified documents

Sonnet branches

The forearm of spring rests on the window sill
to the kitchen where I'm boiling opera for pasta.

This branch of spring is a real interloper,
a man's arm covered in hard yellow blossoms,
No. 2 yellow, like a line of forsythia
in inter-winter-spring. Other sonnet branches
are scattered in the backyard, fourteen limbs
decked out in *the darling buds of May.*
The man's branch intrudes through the open
window in early spring, so it's a line in a poem.

Those italicized and underlined branches
about timeless beauty, a love w/out physical detail,
maybe the pivot toward writing and the writer,
I'll have to pick up after them after dinner,

I'll organize w/ a ladybug red wheelbarrow,
kindling for prose or a Triskelion.

The Battle of Silicon Valley at Daybreak

In a countryside green as a dollar bill,
with the much handled commercial vegetation
from around mall parking lots or in freeway divides,
in a landscape where the wireless has been shut off,
emoji are at war. Emoji are at war
in the mural outside the employee cafeteria
for reading *The Things They Carried* or *Yellow Birds*
or *The Red Badge of Courage*: instead of eating,
emoji are at war.

Outfitted in a list supplied by Wikipedia,
(breastplates, gauntlets, steel collars, mail shirts,
vambrace, pouldron, bassinet, barbute, aventail),
chain armor from a 3-d printer for a smaller budget,
emoji are at war: Blushing Emoji, Frustrated, Weeping,
Smiling Emoji near the village firewall,
& a thousand spears like toothpicks,
emoji are at war.

It's like Where's Waldo. It's like Pac Man.
I spot with my little eye in the "watch-fires of a hundred
circling camps" two generals outside a recharging tent,
a tiny banner unfurling PRIVACY * NET NEUTRALITY
* DEREGULATION. Sound of emoji blood
as the Smiling Emoji advance, swallowing everything,
going postal, kamikaze, road rage, suicide bomber
"hurling down to the House of Death so many sturdy souls,"
sound of emoji blood.

A sword pierces Blushing Emoji #956, Pram's son,
below the groin, and "the dark came whirling down
across his eyes"; a hurled spear is shot through the temple of
Angry Emoji #23, only son of Matthew Thornton
of Boston, and "the dark came swirling thick across his eyes,"
sound of emoji blood. Sound of Emoji blood as Weeping
Emoji #3,418, daughter of the river god, a bullet
plunging into her lung, lodges in the "mortal spot,"
scream fumes.

Outside the village firewall, internet access was slowing
way, *way* down until the CEO who has her eye on Jim,
a Cubicle Emoji, petitions the Board of Directors
to rescue Jim from his jangling fate of war, seduces him,
gives birth to a daughter ½ Hollywood, ½ New Jersey mortal,
with a weak ankle…Emoji were at war.
The CAPS LOCK is on,
so this story ends at the door to the men's restroom.
For we have seen,

I have seen, you have seen, they have seen how emoji blood sounds
like a ring tone of a 50 gun salute in a thousand wavy ploughed
lines, lines, lines, lines where truth is marching on.

Social Media Ensō

Look daily, check every
        20 minutes inside this gate
                of calligraphy made
                        with a single brushstroke
mirror mirror on the wall
        a background of vowels
                o—ohm like eyeholes
                        split screen   ego is lessness
a white scroll for Facebook
        who's the smartest status
                update *sexiest wealthiest*
                        busiest talented of them all
Notice a pattern of skulls
        in the social stationary
                Dead Heads or deadhead
                        a long haul without paying
passengers or freight or
        to ride without buying a ticket
                dead flowers snapped away
                        to encourage others to bloom
with encrypted information
        because you lost your i-
                phone, pod, pad
                        in an underground tomb
& 100,000 early Christian martyrs
        like adults at a sleepover
                see the screen illuminate
                        in the ashen dark

as you send yourself a message
where are you
& try to summon your lost be-
longing from the hotel room
this is no ordinary love
a brushstroke to represent the moment
zeitgeist.

Rhetorical Invention at the Poll

Mister X and the Dream Blog
is also called "Portrait of a Monk Getting New Idea."

Black hairs sprout from chin.
Spanish moss on the side of tarred telephone pole

where a message has been stapled, a poster:
need roommate, need a new religion

& he reads with bloodshot eyes.
A title: Going Public, or Publicity,

A theme: a religious treaty, a lost cat.
Standing behind him is a demon

who wears a necklace of micro aggressions,
past critic on standby power, vampire power,

phantom or ghost load of leaking electricity—
a glowing civilization in the valley ahead,

a troll farm.

Not an Official Communication

the phish is served beside the spam,
the ham salad near the Jell-O mold near the deviled eggs,

Lobster Thermidor in a warmer,
a roast chicken with white bonnets on its leg bones,

a Pepto Bismol pink chiffon cake
on a platter, the foods from foreign lands—

canapé, pu pu platter, bagels, guacamole (pronounced
Gwah-ka-mo-lay we are told), Italian pizza, Welsh Rabbit, Chicken à la King

—dished up w/ a Bundt cake, shrimp cocktail, Watergate salad,
Cheeseburger pie, Baked Alaska, another helping of Watergate salad.

I'd prefer to eat the gleam off these meals
from the 1960s *Betty Crocker*'s *New Picture Cookbook*,

the shiny parentheses, even the backspace.
Watch for common tricks:

the bowl of fruit that's not really a bowl of fruit:
instead it's scratch n' sniff tutti frutti

partisan and the rot of authoritarian
slink under the pile. Basic messages often create

a sense of urgency or fear
by threatening to revoke account access

or pretending to be important notices
from payroll or human resources,

(*e.g.*, it's 6:21 at night, you're still at work,
eating salad in Tupperware at your desk,

your boss emails to say he's in a meeting
and needs to speak with you immediately.

Turns out he needs you to run an errand for him,
buy Amazon gift cards for his son's birthday party).

The recommended serving size changes according to the era.
For example, here's a slice from before the 2016 election:

I was kidnapped. This elephant has been alone for 28 years. Want to get laid? Ride a reindeer to work, Alexandria. Want to fight for wolves in court? Another courtroom win for whales! Add your name if you'll be watching tonight. The next president of the United States. Let's wing this thing. Let's wipe out this killer. This is a partisan witch hunt, Alexandria. Another trick to attack women's health care. For Feminist Friends. Don't leave this until last minute. My brother has schizophrenia. Want to fly out to for the next debate? Let's make history: Add your name. It's time to take back Congress. Rare wolves being hunted out of existence. STEM is for boys and girls. Train wreck. The end for rhinos? This elephant has been alone for 28 years. Be One of 30,000. Hi! Are you single. Flowers in Less Than 2 hours.

& a slice with parsley asterisks from 2018-2019:

Giving Tuesday. Put down that wine bottle. You're one of our biggest supporters. You are a winner. Winner N15887 Please Confirm. Business Deal for You. Work from Home. Progress doesn't happen overnight. Make it One Term. 20% off and free shipping. Shhh Secret Sale inside.

Stand out in a marshmallow world. Last Chance to Get Your Gifts. Should Congress stand up to the NRA? Smarter hiring. Trump's Wall. Elect Women. Halfway to our Goal. You're one of our biggest supporters. Investigation launched. Open this email. Insulin prices. Trump's Twitter. Put down that wine bottle. Your donation record last year. Helpless whales trapped. Cold dogs. Cats Left Out in Cold. Chicken Slaughter. Coyote Whacking. Open this email. Longest Shutdown Ever. Want to run for office?

HOME ECONOMICS

> "Almost every person has something secret he likes to eat. He is downright furtive about it usually, or mentions it only in a kind of conscious self-amusement, as one who admits too quickly, 'It is rather strange, yes—and I'll laugh with you.'"
>
> —M.F.K. Fisher, *Serve It Forth,* 1937

Eliza Leslie plays pinochle
at a card table, Betty Crocker
sits with a TV tray in her lap,
they'll be joined later by Amy
Vanderbilt busy with *vermicelli*
and M.F.K. Fisher in a beret
—annoying the rest with how
she lets the Cold War in—
who wrote *How to Cook a Wolf*
though E.L. boasts she's digitized
by Google, specifically *Directions*
for Cookery in its various branches,
the immensely successful *Seventy-Five Receipts*
in Cakes, Pastry, and Sweetmeats.

A dill plant gone to flower
springs from a crack in the sidewalk
a stack of pastel paragraphs
pistachio and insulation pink
hat box on top of air raid shelter
epochs layered in a parfait glass.
E. L. moves around an Airstream,
Quonset hut, and double-wide trailer
like game pieces while Betty
files Fear, Hope, Love in a box

and cakes parade past on platters,
Orange Satin Ribbon Cake
Sailboat Cake, Lady and Lord
Baltimore Cake on handy tabs.
"As I was saying," E.L.
finishes her lecture on tongue soup,
"be sure that your kitchen girl
thoroughly scrubs turnips."

To wit "America's First Lady of Food"
sings, "I am democratic":

> Open House Menu, page 54
> Kentucky Derby Day, page 46
> On Ike's Farm at Gettysburg, page 46
> Election Night (At Home), page 48
> Fashion Luncheon, page 49
> Party at Mount Vernon, page 58.

Leslie deals a box top, N1, pawn,
certificate of achievement, then a carbon ring,
"The difficulty of preparing cakes
will be great, and in most instances a failure;
involving disappointment, waste of time,
and useless expense. Did you have at hand
marble mortar, hickory rods,
a spaddle or spattle,
little tins for queen cakes?"
I have seen many a wood cooking spoon
stuck in concrete in cul de sacs of housing,
rapid constructions after the war.
Intersection of Pleasantville and Greenfield,
my ankles are too thin for me to walk,
and I certainly do not drive a car

though this neighborhood of pink and green
squares requires a vehicle for motion.

Vanderbilt: Have you tried Emily Dickinson's recipes
for Black Cake, for Coconut Cake
(spices filtered through Hawthorne's custom house)?
Our author's student Dan prepared one
in the exact way of Dickinson,
slant rhyme, too, and received an A.

When we entertained, E.L. continues,
adding "Recipe for Callow Youth" to Crocker's box,
who came over to our Philadelphia house
but George Washington, Thomas Jefferson,
Ben Franklin? My father was a watchmaker.
Mr. Jefferson nominated him a member
of APS (American Philosophical Society).
One year I out-earned Hawthorne in annual income
from writings (my $350 to his $108).
Stretching the meat, spare the sweets,
stretching the milk supply.
I had to sell my receipts when father died.
"Hunger was the only appetizer during the frontier
years," Betty says, but now we have new adventures
in appetizers, deviled eggs, dried beef whirls,
canapés, Hollywood Dunk, Moss Ball,
and bread called a "bagel"
when entertaining Company Men.

We greet husband at the door in his polished shoes
in HINTS TO THE HOMEMAKER:
"Refresh your spirits. Every morning before breakfast,
comb hair, apply makeup and a dash of cologne.
Does wonders for your morale and your family's, too!

Think pleasant thoughts while working and a chore
will become a 'labor of love.' Have a hobby.
Garden, paint pictures, look through magazines
for home planning ideas, read a good book
or attend club meetings. Be interested—
and you'll always be interesting!" Marriage
is the most competitive business in the world.

Vanderbilt: Engagement / Wedding Plans /
Wedding Attire for Women / For Men / Putting Together
the Invitations List / The Wedding Consultant /
The Caterer / The Food, The Cake, The Liquor /
The Honeymoon / Postponing a Wedding / Canceling a Wedding /
The Double Wedding / The Military Wedding /
The Rehearsal / Getting Married Again /
Reaffirmation of Vows / Today's Club Life /
Car Etiquette / Taxi Etiquette / Preserving Family Ties /
The Official Side of Life.
By the by, I was illustrated by Andy Warhol.

Leslie: Abraham and Mary Todd Lincoln bought
Directions in 1846. It went to the White House.

Crocker and Vanderbilt, to Leslie:
"You're a rotund woman who crosses
her too thin ankles under an insulated paragraph."

M.F.K. Fisher, sweet and silent,
who dried pieces of tangerine
on a radiator and found it delicious:
"How to Be Sage
Without Hemlock," "How to Catch the Wolf,"
"How to Distribute Your Virtue," "How to Boil Water,"
"How to Keep Alive," "How to Rise Up Like New Bread,"

"How to Be Cheerful Through Starving,"
"How to Carve the Wolf," "How to Make a Pigeon Cry,"
"How to Pray for Peace," "How to Have a Sleek Pelt,"
"How to Lure the Wolf" as well as "Drink the Wolf,"
and "How Not to Be an Earthworm."

Leslie: "That is, on choosing fresh fish,
select only those who are thick and firm,
with bright gills and stiff fins,
the eyes full and prominent,"
a tremendous profile is much desired.
Slow cooker, how the leaves collect the stars,
the dealer takes the hand,
a double Run in Trump, contrail rebus
of rabbit, diamond, star.

Leslie: "And you, you put pineapple in *everything*."

Crocker: They listened to me intently
over the radio, weekly broadcasts.
A troop of smartly-dressed women at desks
at the Betty Crocker Home Office
answering letters with my signature,
The Betty Crocker Library,
the test kitchens Californian,
Scandinavian, Japanese.
Just follow the Red Spoons.

Fisher, quoting Crocker:
Hot Tuna Salad, Ham Mousse, Crab Louis
Vegetables Bright, Vegetables Gay

Squaw Corn, Cauliflower Porcupine
Far East Eggplant, Parisian Onion Soup

Eggs Florentine, Welsh Rabbit
Maryland, Montana, or Midwest Fried Chicken?

Leslie: Who among us actually married
or ran a household? … except M.F.K.
"We all know how *that* turned out."
"Really?? Did you have to go there?"
heard from behind the Saran-wrapped couch.

Leslie: Many women thought you real, Betty,
though you were a composite of 75 American housewives
who sent in to a contest sponsored
by flour. Even your signature is manufactured.
Pearls, white collars, a touch of
gray to your hair, hoop earrings as concession
to the 1960s, and now soccer mom in
cardigan sweater. The Marlboro Man
or Mr. Clean might be to your taste.
Salisbury steak or Hungry Man's Dinner.

Vanderbilt and Fisher chant:
Like an octopus of cooking pot
or ironing steam, Betty flails
her mop of hair, tentacles with nails
driven into their ends, her pearls clatter
and return to their shells,
she vanishes through a pout.
Now look what you have undone.

Bowl of Fruit

set in front though slightly to the left of
the wide stripes of lowered window blinds
made from the repetition of a statement
in dot-matrix and in Constantia,
a genre not meant to be actually read,
a user's agreement or prescription disclaimer,

this fruit is made with a stamp.
...lemon, grapes, apple lemon grapes apple
lemon, grapes, lemon grapes apple pear
grapes, lemon grapes grapes apple pear [1]

The rest of the penthouse is a taped-on list
in a manual: the back wall is a full-page infomercial,
the door is a travel brochure, the foreground
a telephone book, the windows an online review,
and the peephole is taken from a bestselling mystery.
A wine glass from a yellowed advertisement
for a sale on crystal is taped near a black & white houseplant,
a Boston fern from page 18 near the Sports Section.
A ghostwritten accent chair. Click on the chaise lounge.
Blinding white, patterned, busy, hypnotic.
A sculpture of a question mark is in the mirror.
Yellow sentences crisscross the room
POLICE LINE DO NOT CROSS.

Under the headline near the couch,
a face has fallen onto the carpet
from a pedestal made from a Roman numeral:
priest / cowboy / general / dictator,
stereotypes already leak from his head in No. 2 red.

Cleft chin, Adam's apple, widow's peak,
the not-included six-pack, stubble.
No mention in the report of the expensive stereo system,
but that doesn't prove anything.
The Benday dots in the five o'clock shadow
of his rugged handsomeness
(like the large pores on a lemon,
like a bulleted list, like satellites
abandoning ship) drift off and fade the room:

- you should've stopped
- when you were ahead. // Yield to power. //
- To others pass authority like a peach. //
- Roll with it, run with it // on ceiling glass.

[1] lemon, grapes, apple lemon grapes apple
each a nude in a bowl, tired of being a nude in a bowl,
finally did something about it, lemon, grapes,
apple lemon grapes apple, apple pear:
first name apple, last name pear.

Poem with I VOTED Sticker

What color would you say is on those pink walls in that apartment,
third floor, a desk lamp like a spotlight, like an interrogation lamp,
no one around? Would you say it's powderpuff pink, pink paradise,
pale pink satin, blushing brilliance, pink canopy, orchid pink,
rosetta, sharon rose, primrose, conch shell, crazy for you, nautilus
shell, flamingo, rosebud, forever young, cameo rose, rose lace,
pink panther, cotton candy, unspoken love, princess, prom dress,
rose rococo, engagement, tippy toes, hearts delight, secret garden,
marry me, fantasy pink, venetian rose, countryside pink, misty
rose, secret rendezvous, pretty in pink, bed of roses, ballet slippers,
sweet 16, baby's mittens? You're right as usual, you certainly know
your stuff, you're an authority in all matters, you know best, I defer
to your judgment, you're practically omniscient, I am a vessel for
your wisdom, you're my sage on the stage, I'm often told I'm a good
listener. It's not bed of roses, rose mist, or Florida pink. As you & I
stroll by, our hands stapled together, pedestrians walking past homes
with poems like this one on desks, lists like graffiti on stanzas walls,
what should we do about it, why not buy a goddamn big car, if I
VOTED stickers interrupt lists in stanzas, on walls?

Still Life with a Blue Narrator

who hides behind a cobalt blue water pitcher
b/c an early draft of this poem was done in the ink of melancholy.
Imp, satyr, possibly a cupid or a boy who needs a haircut,
maybe the small woman w/ a mullet who models
for the poem painter in a rent controlled apartment
who hides behind a kitchen table covered in the begonia
of the first-person, third-person geranium—
pungency of broken leaves, clippings of phrases
in hard to read shadows and murky water.
The navy first-person witness grows from a tendril teal third-person
who hides at the interface of representation and abstraction
in a rent controlled apartment with un-Polish-ed silverware
a survivor's heap of Old World kitchen gadgets
a monogrammed bowl of fruit, a tattooed kitten,
total word count in that dish.
Who hides and is followed up by a radiant blast of responsibility, of omni-
science:
why aren't they assuming more of a leadership role?
Why would an adult narrator play hide and seek
or a federal court judge cower in a houseplant forest?

Incident of Happiness at Rue Straße

The villa of the balcony of words
@ hotel description, www. motel narration.

The villa of the balcony of words
with a railing in cast iron cursive.

Along the roof top in clay pots
perch topiary of bird-shaped connotations,

Mansard roofs on paragraphs
as far as the eye can see &

more writing on the warehouses
& the empty start-ups,

i.e.: the table of contents
nutritional information, a barcode,

& recommended serving size
taped to the outside of buildings.

From the villa of the balcony of words,
we put "money" in the telescope

to find the old shopping mall
of Walter Benjamin's *Arcades*

or the Airbnb your family is renting,
gaze at crosses, tv antenna, swallows & other symbols.

I live close by, over there, near page 58,
near Tru Valu, Bella Vita, Weitblick & Frieden,

across from CAFÉ UMLAUT
and the penciled-in building

and this poelding, the longest under construction:
2001, 2003, 2004, 2013, 2018, 2019,

an italicized building, where I met my husband.

You can reach me at balconyofwords@gmail.com.
On our balcony of words, we highlight

a tourist rolling a suitcase, a boy carrying bread,
& a woman walking a poodle that's ½ a word

along a graphite alley in the double-spaced sector
near the morning markets. A summer sigh moves

a Post-It note stuck to a two-story preposition
on the north side, near the singed cathedral:
- A woman steps out
Where there used to be a balcony,
Onto one of the words which used to describe her,
A word which will not be heard during this poem,
And so she never falls.

Construction Site

In the long-lined poem,
                    a cloud is pierced by the sentence of a girder

Far below is a yellow double-spaced house
          with a college-ruled garage

a scrap of paper
          blows up against the house & becomes a load-bearing wall

In the stratosphere, a heart with an arrow
                    passes between line breaks

pauses over daffodils and rebar

So! In a long-lined yard there's a short-lined garden
                    with a trellis for black roses,

notes or a grocery list, and when vowels of wind
                    press against the house,

a psalm is left on the kitchen counter
                    looked back longingly and was turned into a pillar of salt

Then the poetic line breaks into two and the last half pivots
like an immense piece of construction machinery

changing the direction of this poem
                    transforming it into a recipe, a scientific journal article
                    a memorandum, this Young Adult romance adventure novel

Balsam

This woods made by a stamp
a stamp used throughout
the same words over and over,
gold bulbs and balsam,
calligraphy from the holidays,
woods used to make a stamp
on that piece of air time-date stamped
words used in a stamp

a 300- or 400-word count in/for the woods.
A woods made of stumps
that prop up paintings in ornate frames
the same image over and over:
3 thick bright green lines,
apple-green syllogism and evergreen haiku,
every sixth painting by Neil Welliver
of the woods *used to make a poem*

a 400-word decoy   in the woodsy
art inside art.   When a poem appears
inside another poem   every sixth image
in a postage-stamp sized frame
leaning against the line breaks
is a cartoon of a laughing woman
or a self-taught painting of a 6-point Doe
as the wood duck escapes over a distant copper pond:

A few screw-on scents—No Trespassing,
No Hunting
No Snowmobiling—thrown in.

Overcast, Recast

A mimeographed mountain (a mimeographed mountain)
            from a valley of pencil-yellow-and-lavender is reduced
to cylinders / cones / cubes: Rick Steves & Erle Loran stand
around the copier machine…when a poem w/ ledges of cloud
in a valley of lavender & forsythia on the cover of a travel guide
leads to paragraphs with blasting holes / chisel marks

stanzas w/ quarry marks in a landslide of boxes in the backroom
… the kind paper towels & diapers are shipped in, good for
building castles, playing house, like the brown barnacle
of a castle high up on the side of the poem—as we hike to
the "castle in the clouds" instead of breaking down boxes

& flattening ideas in analysis & synthesis & below:
the yellow & purple paneled valley, tabs of a village,
i.e.: the copy shop, convenience store. A weather front
is moving in, ½ way up—*stamped prices, prize-in-every-box,*
candy asterisks, stone cloud covered in fossilized footnotes.

Landscape @ Aix, at Sidney, Maine

with a Large Pine and Red Earth (1890-95), (1984-2020),
Rocks at Fontainebleau (1893), Mont Sainte-Victoire with Large Pine (1887)
Large Bathers, Bathers at Rest, Belgrade Lakes, Mont Vernon,
the bog, quarry. GPS coordinates of Aix-en-Provence: 43° 31' 47.071"
N 5° 26' 50.737" E. Sidney, ME: 44.45341° N, -69.73702° E.

on sandstone layers of *American Poetry Review,*
Journal of American Poetry, American Poetry Journal,
then *North American Review, New American Writing,*
American Literary Review (on hiatus), Mid-American Review,
New American Writing for me, Scripture for you.
I'm interested in what happens behind the bough of a sentence.
Let's hang out on this blank [unwritten] area

Blocks of sky   quarry of gray and beige tabs
—titles,   sub-titles in craggy heaps
w/ blast marks   the mountain made from 12 mountains:
Faith that moves mountains, for even if you say to this mountain,
"Be taken up and cast into the sea," it will happen, thorn and thistle
aloe and lavender, or pine and birch *growing on their altars,*
they will say to the mountains, "Cover us," and to the hills, "Fall on us."
Sunlight is like a fallen rock   the viper of judgment
at the bottom of the (Corinthians 6:14) ravine (James 4) shaft.

Boughs featherygreen
fields overlapping in connotation   though the sky is chipped
Perched on a ledge of the *Paris Review*, the *Paris-American*
            on a clear day, we can see

- Ferrante's Elena & Lila playing w/ dolls in Naples,
- the stream where Emile Zola & Paul Cezanne swam,
- the midnight blue pond covered in our handwriting.

My tree has two pine cones, yours has six. Soon you'll have grandchildren.
What happens behind the bough of this sentence
as we scramble over rocks into the future. Last weekend,
I watched your son's wedding on Zoom.

Tree of Cones

To let the relationship grow organically,
stacks of detail, pyramids of faces
pointing either upward or downward
as wood-paneled family rooms hang
off branches of *How long*
will I be able to know you?, hard to tell
serving both, the bronze bells needing
polishing. Certain leaves yellowed
no matter the time of the year.

The Mountain That Took The Place

No longer listening to the soprano of loneliness
like an iceberg sailing in the previous sky

picking my way between couplets of rocks
pines returned to their original position

½ way down, I meet a bulky man unlikely hiker
portly insurance man but hear him first, his iambic muttering

forty years before another bulky man on the same path
leaving his studio carrying a chair and sketch pad

In a cairn in reverse direction
the first stanza-paragraph is balanced at the top

a descent that is an ascent
until I reach the base of words on the desk

a landslip of syllables at the bottom of the draft
off in the distance, a one-page mountain

a monadnock is an isolated small poem
rising abruptly from the peneplain in everyone

The same cloud passes overhead

above the subtitle of a sunrise
over a city made entirely of dots.

A standard cumulus but still imposing
yellow tower of thought
on the double spaced atmosphere
over the cliff face of a stanza,
hanging over an immense vault
of unused page space—

"The same cloud passes overhead"

Drive-by cloud,
over a torrent of leaves
and the blush of dawn.

—Cloud crossing two time zones while carrying
a stone arch—

Not the "docile clarity" of the cloud
from Francis Ponge's "The Insignificant,"
—more as pastiche, appropriation, parody,
simulation, adaptation, recycling—
an emissary from *Against Expression,*
Unoriginal Genius, or *Uncreative Writing.*

By the end, the cloud occurs so often it becomes unfamiliar,
a *could,* a decrescendo
in white hallways to tomorrow,
zig zag sunset.

Another Landscape Poem

Poem-within-a-poem means driving around the staple,
avoiding the storm-within-storm, heading deeper into
the white countryside of Possibility, a straw village,
a stone village, in the midlands at midlife,
a farming region where there are no orchards &
but always orchards because of the transparent hand erasing
redrawing jittery trees until the reclusive rental cottage,
the tone poem stone wall in the fold-out section:
        poem stone wall
        tone stone poem
        made of sea glass
        one round sound ™
        stacked on pale blue
        beer brown agiorpe
        aphid green sound
, in milkweed, in queen anne's lace
with the peppery smell of rented bowling shoes, in cornflower,
chamomile, lamb's ear, thistle, parking meters of sunflowers;
among Latin italics, botanical names for spriggy plants
from "Spring and All" ,,, rusting plants from "The Rite of Spring"
thawing plants from Andrew Bird : you have arrived at your /
the farm stand. Be the first to review this item:
- a page number on the property line / [a fallow field]
<not to be overworked, over
thought> if you select the portrait view.

Hills of Bureaucracy

In the event
that the engagement
shall be prevented
by reason of war,
Act of God, strike,
civic tumult, epidemic
or any other cause
beyond the control
of either agreeing party,
which is deemed
to be "force majeure,"
the agreed parties
shall be respectively
relieved of their obligations
contained herein and
return to the rolling hills
of bureaucracy,
a deep green field
of barley, more hills
with hay bales, no sky:
an argyle of crops,
following emergency exits
and evacuation plans
to *the long and winding*
road that leads
to your door.

That would be 15 A
on the updated form,
the red door
with a mat and rack

for your shoes
of a cottage in the village.
Let the minutes state
you've had a tiresome
journey through various causes
on the lengthy lavender road
past blaze orange fields
that shall include revolutions,
riots, wars, acts of enemies,
national state local
emergency, strikes,
floods, fires, epidemics,
quarantine, embargoes,
or unusually severe weather,
and that we're not responsible
or liable for any loss
or damage, for delays
in performance
or failure to perform.
The 10 point font path
has brought you to the Open Forum
on Comprehensive
Internationalization,
where the committee
invites input from the whole
community about where
we are at and where
we should go,
which thatched houses
for which gas stations
in the settlements of
educational plans, mission
statements, internal hiring.
The designated spokesperson

from the institutional
advancement office is explaining:
This is a plan for all
of us. A family reunion
hosted by Human Resources
in partnership
with Business Intelligence,
Focus on Core Academic Function,
so the member
at the back of the conference room
knitting wooly yarn clouds
as stress relief
should get a grip.
We've all stopped
our planting in favor
of administering to
attend this conference
on the administration of planting,
Cc: all: the assistant to, vice-,
associate, interim, acting,
chief, head of, associate director.
Staples for vineyards.
Collated construction
plans are in departmental
mail boxes. Approving
the minutes from yesterday,
let's send the next presenter back
like a salmon stunned w/ frustration
who weeps with frustration
into the whirling vortex
of a policy about policy,
a few hay bales,
shade trees for cattle
or the sub-committee to

this committee,
though Party 1 is not a fish
but a person who must drive
back in his rental Kia,
the application form
was incomplete.
Next order of business:
those ornamental wild
grasses planted
last year for the parade,
tall, on the highway divide
on Route 2 South,
junction of JFK Boulevard
and South Main,
a deathtrap or death wish?

Title covered in flies

Flies that in a previous life were horses in a field,
work horses, winking and flicking their tails
under an omniscient horse chestnut tree
so close in those green hallways to the next
appointment of strong reactions. Full circle
what I dislike, even despise, at some point

I was, I did, and the tree's rope swing untethers,
sways in small expanding circles, hypnotizing
tobacco-stained slats of a barn, aligning needles of hay.
Green fires that were fly-covered horses in a field.
We reject ourselves
beside the ruins of a farm house
                                        not ready to burn itself down.

Landfill Basics, The White Paper

dis	pos	able	dis	pos	able				
dis	dis	pos	able	dis	pos				
pos	pos	pos	dis	dis	dis				
pos	dis	able	pos	dis	pos				
				Bic	pen	45-	60	%	45%
				40-	60%	60	%	CH_4	CH_4
				CH_4	CH_4	CH_4	CH_4	CH_4	CH_4
				CO_2	CO_2	CO_2	CO_2	CO_2	CO_2
CH_4	CH_4	CO_2	CO_2	CH_4	CH_4				
CH_4	CH_4	CH_4	CH_4	CH_4	CH_4				
CO_2	CO_2	CO_2	lap	top	com				
puter	CO_2	CH_4		CH_4	CO_2				
				dif	dif	dif	dif	dif	dif
				us	ion	us	ion	us	us
				dif	dif	desk	lamp	us	ion
				dif	ill	usio	n il	us	ill
sm	all	er	er	er	er				
er	er	er	er	er	ma				
er	er	er	it	a	to				
am	ou	nts	to	sm	er				
				ain	air	ain	air	ain	air
				ain	air	ain	~~air~~	air	ain
				air	air	ain	bloated hill		ain
				air	air	air	air	ain	air

municipalsolidwastelandfillsmunicipalsolidwastelandfillsmunicipal-
solidwastelandfillsmunicipalsolidopendumpsopendumpsopendump-
sopendumpsopendumpsopendumpsopendumpsopendumpsopen-
dumpconstructiondemolitionlandfillconstructiondemolitionlandfill-
constructiondemolitionlandfillconstructiondehazardouswastevegeta-
tionwasteanimalwastehazardouswasteanimalwastehazardouswaste-
animalwastehazaopendumpsopendumpsopendumpsopendumpsopen-
dumpsopendumpsopendumpsopendumpsopendumpsconstruction-
demolitionlandfillconstructiondemolitionlandfillconstructiondemoli-
tionlandfillconstructionhazardouswastevegetationwasteanimalwasteh-
azardoushazardouswastevegetationwasteanimalwastehazar

till	ation	poi	nt	gap	cra	ck
flo	or	ga	p	crac	cra	ven
t	win	dow	in	drai	n	ack
ga	p	ven	t	en	try	point.

Ring Tones

Black branch of footsteps overhead
giggle-colored blossoms along a sleeve

the flowers are typed on the kimono
Glenn Gould mumbled, left marks above

Bach and Mozart, that inlaid forest
of topaz and ruby and emerald

I pull a peel-away strip of diacritics
from over a mother & son at the kitchen counter

a band of stick figures dancing
inside the long-division problem

smoky italics above the hills
sunflowers like cushions along the couch

bright threads of chickadeebluejaygoldfinchcardinal
in a needlepoint of a porch gone winter-white

branch of footsteps overheard in the woods
quotation marks around a single leaf it rings like a bell

The Recording

If I press that area in the poem, a poem filling with small circles & set in a polished oak holder, if I press that area, the future plays from red or blue-rimmed ovals & oblongs in a stack, like frames around leaves.

In a canopy of empty picture frames, my daughters lean into the compressed white forest-city. I know they stand on the other side, tall women laughing gently at their mother at 41, 42, 43 as I listen to the wall. Silly woman that I was, who spent so many hours in this room with paper walls.

If I shake this poem, give it a really sound shake, putting little " " marks around all of it to show movement, I hear a colored gravel of sounds. It forms a kaleidoscope reader. (Twists of blankets) at the end of the long tube, *small bowls for cereal* at the far end of a long tunnel. (Track 44) (the cursive voice interrupted) (the cursive voice recorded over), the voice pressed like a violet in an old book.

Little, Chipped

At a mostly empty hole-in-the-wall, a black curtain over the door. Looking for the first signs of people, the yard curling upward. It's too cold to be sitting outdoors so long, your digits growing numb. No one to tell you to come inside. You wear your father's fisherman sweater, a big, thick thing your mother knitted when they met, and you hold a tea cup between both palms and blow across it. Contents provided by the cold stove in the room behind, the linoleum peeling upward.

A quick sketch of spring, first signs, that's what you'll say if they show up. Just a detail on an elaboration, a thickening, a wavy form growing forward, that's your explanation to those who approach with an orchid between their eyes.

Chopin Nocturne No. 2 in E Flat, Op. 9, No. 2

In the dream footage I climb over broken furniture
that didn't survive, high-backed chairs embroidered
in song birds, ottomans and office chairs, conference tables
desks locked with flimsy keys, filing cabinets of the rococo
over a heap of documents no one would ever start
no one would ever finish, on the industrial carpet below
17,136 lanyards became alpine flowers at a memorial
for everyone attended by no one, my movements were
out of synch with the soundtrack and in the baroque window
in the modern park, trees made strange dances that pandemic
spring bereft of leaves, across the town commons
I could see the marble stairs to the Institute of Institutions

—where I'd once put in an application
—they were barely passable, seemed covered in buildings
—a ruined farmhouse, a college hidden in ivy
—The Grand Hotel, its second floor filled with broken furniture
—where a tiny sleepwalker pantomimed climbing
—more buildings with blankets tossed over them
—towers domes gothic spires under those blankets.

How I Was Raised

A toy plank on a desk
beside the "S" volume from
the Encyclopedia Britannica
(Dale Carnegie's *How*
to Win Friends behind
plastic ivy on the toilet tank
crochet cover on Kleenex box)
in a living room of self-taught

Art or art.

A plank is like a desk
but at this incline, intuition is scattered
—red rubber balls,
points along a line,
run-over thoughts of stars—
and a window left open at the top
so a flock of instincts
silver flash in the ceiling.

Five Per Page

Autobiography of a Lazy Boy Recliner

Yard sticks and shards are kept in a jar shaped as a cowboy boot. Snapped hours stand in a drywall bucket along with a nineteen inch glare in a hot attic. Can you guess how many errors this jar contains? How many agnostic gumballs? How many tangerine parking garages? Does it contain at least one broom closet for diminishing mascots? Suddenly I'm calling the name of my childhood best friend. Rachelerika! Rachelerika! In an evaporated place, the dotted lines scatter.

The Sears Painting That Hangs Over the Recliner

I am made from many stanzas put together, blank stanzas, canvases stapled. With ellipsis.

Braided Rug

Swirl vortex whorl made by a grandparent of silence is placed under a Sears art thrift store painting, smiley face yellow.

The School Project

Volcano on cushion of kitchen chair is paper mâché. Pistol on paper plate under cash register is real.

Book Report, "Growing Up in a Convenience Store"

Your job is to open that which is delivered with a box cutter. Offer includes *Jubilat Agno,* the Care-free, Payless, Payday, Pop Rocks, the whatchamacallit, the 100 Grand, Charleston Chew, Swedish fish for a penny, chewable astronauts, Can eat the spoon, Lik-A-Stix. Offer excludes the yellow slide of childhoodhoodchild along with the *doors of perception*. Limit of 2 Haiku per box, per customer:

A frog covered with dust
emerging from the candy rack
scares a bitter customer.

Shadowbox

In a catalog of shadowboxes, a recliner, braided rug, taped-on window, fireplace.

A gloved hand will appear, hover over the list.

The recliner is forest green with a lever for lowering or raising one's position,

a cascade of mountain flowers in the throw-blanket, a stack of conversations like already-read magazines beside the cut-out brass poker.

The gloved hand pushes apart two commas, makes more room.

In a shadow's box, a recliner, circular rug, reading lamp, cobra, and fireplace.

An avalanche of alpine flowers (//) spills into a novel by Murakami or Saknussemm

for a book report lying face down as a cone of light interrogates the back of the chair

with a view of the paper mâché volcano at the science fair.

The gloved hand moves to the end of the catalog.

Round and round on the rug, the centipede time line circles the Lazy Boy.

It drags centuries of pictures from a man's life as little boxes attached to its legs *like a parade dragon.*

GREENFIELD, U.S.A.

> *"Today is a special day in Greenfield. There is a parade. There will be a party. Here comes a parade! It is coming along Main Street. See the big cake on the jeep! It is Greenfield's birthday cake. There is almost enough cake for everyone at the party."*

It starts with a chewable sidewalk,
half a dozen Springfields in every direction
fewer Greenfields, tv antenna and church spires
pastel siding on the buildings of the social sciences
(geography, history), a school's program of green days
turning yellow. Long blank stretches left for streets
in *A New Hometown*, where Ted and his family
have just moved. In the early hours,
a station wagon—fishing poles, plaid shirts,
matching windbreakers—Ted and his father
pass the radio repair shop, the drive-thru,
Greenfield Bank, Wilson's Department Store,
On Main Street and ACE CAFE where the fry-cook
(all occupations underlined) in checked paper hat
refills a cup for Joe, who repairs cars
like Bobby's father's car, he DELIVERS THE MAIL.
The station wagon will break down
in a minor way in a few paragraphs. Citizens of trim waists
wave as Ted and his father pass:
1966 © D. C. Heath and Company.

*

On instinct, Mike looks up from studying the watercolor plains
(this is middle America), green/brown/blue quadrants

of sky divided into various grade school subjects,
sees *Four Lands, Four Peoples* way off
but before that *A New Hometown* and its water tower
that sends signals about the number of views,
time spent per page. Farther away but before
the spine of the mountain range,
A Course for Composition and Rhetoric
by G. P. Quackenbos, *McGuffey's New Fourth Eclectic Reader,*
grid of brown and gold with mildew blooms
that could be dried blood, this copy carried
in a breast pocket during the Civil War, taken out
for Samuel Smiles-style self-improvement
during haphazard hours thrown down by campfire.

*

Yes, says Mary. Yes, says Sally. Yes, says Ted,
but not Betty, Ted's mother, at the Formica kitchen table
in her bathrobe and lipstick, drinking coffee and smoking
Pall Malls (this part edited out). We see the Bundt cake
with long-stemmed dandelion growing from a crack.
She will wear slacks to plant the sapling in the front yard
of their new home while the puppy dances
like a Sufi (see glossary). Mike waves to Sally,
the new neighbor across the street.
Her father DELIVERS THE MAIL.
And Mike thinks thoughts of her, none in Times 14 font.
He sips his Tang, continues copying:
The Importance of Social Studies
"The importance of social studies can
hardly be overestimated. Our society
is highly efficient in many branches
of technology, from the manufacture
of essential goods to the science of destruction."

Between 1976 and 1979, we spent hours playing school
while our parents worked in our country store:

> Behind the walk-in coolers and inside the storage room my brother, sister, and I play school while our parents tend the counter… We recognized customers by their voices and stayed in the shadows like minnows in the darker depths around a fallen tree if the customers were uninteresting or if the interaction unharmonious. The clatter of the cash register and lines of dialog were audible all day. As the oldest, I play the teacher. To start the lesson, I raise the top of one of the antique school desks in our playroom. Like an enormous tadpole, a disco-gold comma is inside the desk, completely covering the out-of-date textbook, bought at a yard sale as a toy. In the same way, a giant water bug had appeared in a tank of summer creatures we'd gathered, all the tadpoles suddenly gone. (page 6)

And in the rooms of university offices
the textbook representatives come and go
singing of sample essays about Michelangelo.
Almost everyone in Greenfield is at the parade.
Who do you think is working?
Sally's brother will be blown up
in a place not included in the index
of *Four Lands, Four Peoples*.
Sally will attend Wesleyan and live with women in a yurt:
Boston/Englewood/Chicago/San Francisco/Atlanta/Dallas.

*

At the back of the poem, so much unused,
well-lit space, property lots that start behind the words,
not the same as space between words.
It's the pasture where images are given medallions,
where sensations are parked with a hmmmm.
Turn the poem to one side, three seconds of iridescence,
and for a few moments nothing appears
until—*wait for it, wait for it*—you make out
pink skyscrapers of the future perfect tense
like enormous bouncy houses tied down
in a few seconds of micro distance.
Clouds await the return of the schoolmaster
or a mother's note. A few passing pterodactyls
mingle with hang gliders, with the municipal airport
so nearby, so adds Ted, oh that Ted, in the margins
of the school book. A man herding blobs ...
followed by farm animal sounds made by toys.
Militants' propaganda billboards
lord over a quadrant of the quiz space.
The reader is now invited to pull a few italicized steps
from the poem like a hide-away bed
and expand upon the last few lines, adding images,
objects from his [sic] immediate surroundings.

*

fr.—Fret, frog, fred, from, fril, frend, fry, frute, frunt,
fresh, frame, fro, free, fra.
10. A large number of monkeys will sometimes get
together, in the morning, in the woods. One of them
will seat himself, and begin a speech, while the rest
will keep silent.
INTERJECTIONS, or words used to denote a sud-
den emotion of the mind; as, *ah! alas! O! oh! fie! hist!*

11. When he has done, they all set up a shout, as
if for applause, and then the monkeys disperse.
FOR DISCUSSION: Do you think Egypt might be interested
in buying machines made in Switzerland?
Have one of the children find out and report
on the life of Rudolph Diesel.
Discuss the idea that skill can add value to
chemical raw materials. FOR DISCUSSION:
Tell two ways in which a cloud may disap-
pear. ANSWER "USING CLUES."
PRESENTATION: Have the children read to the heading "Border
Problems." Words newly used are *broadcasting*
and *official*. Not in index: Soviet Union or Vietnam
though on map, pages 222-223,
India and Her Neighbors. Suggested Films:
Balloons in the Sky. 36 minutes, color, Swiss
National Tourist Office.

*

: watercolor plains

green/brown/blue quadrants

grade school subjects,

Four Peoples way off

water tower

number of views,

carefully:

-shire
-ester
-town
-ville.
-murals
of De Chirico, Klee, Miro
(Betty is flipping through an art folio)

can be discovered in the alley behind the BAKERY
near BRYER'S HARDWARE
Tools & Paint, after *Reliable Electric Corp.*,
after BROWN'S GARAGE.
#6 on the door plate
on one of the pink peeling drafts
as an arm like a tattoo of a tree branch
but with the speed of the Metro
moves past, adding triangles of detail.

An electric-blue carp swims like a neon sign
in the river of Greenfield, Greenfield River.
Mike looks up from the model of the airport he's building.
Sally looks down at the shadowbox she's making,
adding a cot, a trailer, a piece of skyscraper.

Under a broadband sunset, after-school oak leaves
in a heap like faded wrappers from classical candy bars.
100 Grand, Charleston Chew, Payday, Pound, Eliot.
Instead of bugs, soft flannel geometric shapes spring
out of the tall grass beside the road,
to land on a chewable sidewalk.

Junk Drawer

Pull the command verb handle on a rectangular poem lined
with contact paper, dots and dashes like a crop picked over,
a corn maze already deciphered, where once rows of rhyming plants,
the unwanted items from a flea market closed for the season:
a crumplednoun and the melted stub of a 1943soldier—a flip phone—
Aloha!—coins with your parents' faces—a child's name you decided
not to use—a receipt for reincarnation. No bin separating details,
one or two similes slide (hard) into the upper right hand corner.

Gloved and Wingéd Hand at Edge of Paragraph

… Chapstick applied. Drawer closed. Coffee cup raised. Drawer open. Song changed. Song returned to. Drawer closed. Chapstick applied. Pen cap put on. Another pen picked up. Coffee cup raised. Desk chair pushed back and coffee cup brought into the kitchen. Door opened. Full coffee cup slid on desk an inch beyond surface area covered in Post-Its. Space heater dial lowered. Door closed. Drawer open. Coffee cup raised, then lowered, then raised quickly again. Pen bouquet in shot glass reshuffled. Chapstick applied. Drawer closed. Door opened. Pages rifled. Pen cap removed. Chapstick applied. Song returned to. Song returned to. Space heater dial raised. Door opened and closed. Song changed. Drawer closed. Coffee cup raised and lowered. Slid off. Smearing important words on a pink Post-It. Pen cap removed. Space heater turned off. Door opened. Water glass slid next to coffee cup. Water glass raised, lowered. Chapstick applied.

Ouroborus

A piece contains a sentence with a certain number of nouns and a certain number of verbs in an admixture with other parts of speech. Some are color coded pink, others yellow or pastel green: causing this banded sentence to pass. It races alongside the next sentence and pretends to be a humble underline until the first nips the tail of the later one, ordering it to move faster, start the ball rolling, precisely that round remainder the first sentence has left behind through the course of its action. Or it could be the reverse, that the second and newer sentence turns around to bite its predecessor in the tail, unfairly, because by now the first sentence is worn out, fading, a few seconds older than the second, and rudely, because the newer one is dependent on its ancestor for its existence. An immature sentence may pretend ignorance, but it will not be unaware of this rule because it passed a sentence diagram on the cave wall. On the occasion of which we speak, the best account is that the first sentence turns around in a quick almost imperceptible movement before starting its leg of the race. It makes a grab for its own dark apple, its single offering to the world after it has said its piece, spoken freely, a decimal point suggesting that it's related to what comes after it, in the same phylum, like a semicolon of an eye with tooth might.

Study for a Portrait No. 1 and No. 6

Is that lava or hunks of cold anger on your lower lip?
Why do gritty tents of her grief end up in my mouth?
Spider trees and wind-eaten ponies, spent bullet casings
or the gold hoops that supported the breathing of others
in front of each tooth like flowers at a curbside memorial.
A fence of toothpicks runs up down the contours of
a reclining landscape, shipwrecked olive trees, vineyard-desert.
I'm noticing… I'm noticing…

****

1\. Diptych or triptychs are available at Hotel Francis Bacon
2\. Burnt orange or umber rooms in a double or triple
3\. Spires of a canopy bed in Room A, a carpet of nails
1\. Bullet proof glass box for the defendant on trial
2\. For humanity in Room C, pea green, globally warmed
3\. I am pressing the "move to cart" & "make purchase" button
2\. Oysters couples on platform beds, cow carcass on a crucifix
3\. The third room left purposefully blank for Crimes Against
1\. Silence is not empty for it doth team in squirming shapes
3\. The spires of the cathedral heavily bombed in Room A
1\. Near the maw of the bed, the maw of the subject's mouth
2\. To be talking with someone and see their skull like wet shell
2\. Subject, verb, object dissolving on the heavy tongue
3\. Was this an interrogation or a romance?
1\. A muscle left on an oriental carpet, a reflex on the plaid symphony
3\. Inspiration from iconography upside down, Cimabue's *Crucifixion*
3\. For several years I spotted his Francis Bacon torso
3\. In the driver's seat of other cars, at major intersections
3\. On the floor in rooms whose doors were closed as I passed
2\. A shawl made from pieces of a shroud across shoulders

2. “You bobble head, you dictator”

3. In a ballroom gown of khaki

1. Lure of the expensive sound system… romantic music

2. Hands on e-shopping cart, we should all be on trial

3. Drizzled   breeding other / images

1-3. Yet the rooms peeling like an orange, I veer at the last mo
ment

Portrait Surrounded by Fictional Elements

The scream bubble, broadcast bubble,
icicle bubble, the he said/she said,
the close-captioned and the whisper
balloon, a light bulb balloon,
thought balloons in emotional stripes,
green envy, red rage, blue serenity:

Dog-eared conversations like the copies
of *National Geographic* and *Reader's Digest*
with curled corners in the magazine rack
as *fireplace* is repeated like a brick
and the wood paneling is drawn in with a
subject-verb-object sentence, followed by
a braided rug that wanders in circles.
Amateur paintings of deer and a beige mountain
over which an umlaut cloud passes.
Plot wise, Did something awful happen
in this pine green Lazy Boy in this hunting lodge?

Nothing so awful as not bothering to know each other.
Not visiting, even at the corner of death.
Meanwhile, a voice drips from a faucet
and the salmon pink sentence, doe brown sentence,
moose gray sentence, the duck, the loon sentence,
the coyote and fox sentence, loop around the room,
avoiding corners, a meaningless border.

Portrait Surrounded by Artistic Devices

An adjacency resume, chronological letter, memo,
query, timeless letter, certificate of achievement,
brochure 2-fold, 3-fold, PowerPoint, report—
like clip art used as hotel art, heaps of templates,
hollowed-out mountains in a landscape painting

are displayed on the wall over Bob the odalisque,
who reclines across a burlap couch under a title
borrowed from David Hockney that doubles as a shelf
and holds transparent genre, glitter star of a metaphor.
                                        In a sanded-down bathrobe,
Bob is the portrait of a poem, his head a polished gold
ball on Tu/Ths. His partner is the triangle near Roman drapery
[after the line break] in the corner. Something more specific
stands on the floor, leaning along the sofa:
- framed print of Hockney's "A Bigger Splash 1967"
- annunciation with a lily taken from a lobby
- unframed canvas, "Life Change While in a Hospital Bed"

in which a shaft of motes visits a cranked-up hospital bed
if a person is oblivious to a parallel life passing
near them, or the enormous crack in the floor, a ravine,
a zig zag of thought, a crack that started in a previous poem
and continued thru several stories and monographs.

.A Bigger Splash, -
after David Hockney

A bigger splash equals an !!! a few yards outside a sentence.
It's a straight shot along that dirty yellow sentence, quick dash
down a poetic line—to dive into boxed California cyan-blue
. Our bystander's attention drawn
to a plume of actionreaction like punctuation at the other end,
emphasis at the start as we watch others have fun while we keep
our clothes on, the way European men in suits or Speedos look:
2 palm trees who are a couple walk up the driveway
to the pool party, a canvas director's lawn chair,
LA water, 1 or 2 PM, East Coast time
& a flash-forward of what's coming up behind us

—city skyline at sunset, repressive and drizzly,
reflected in the giant windows of a salmon pink house box
with crawling shrubbery? Soon other typographic devices
arrive, literary agents, a private detective, characters
of the catering staff, pool attendant, the real owner of this house, *!@%!?#!!
plates of Triscuits with Lawrence Welk spray-on cheese & G&T
& the poem naps on a deck chair & w/ a terrific tan
in skivvies or a bra and panty set white as a flash
while the picture frame runs pinkish squares around us
!@%!?#!!!@%!?#!! without yapping.

Portrait with Architectural Elements on a Shelf

The collector puts examples of wainscoting, sills, eaves, cornice
high on a shelf, on the ledge of a sentence, lines as shelves

- so it's like riding in a car and only seeing the upper stories
(penthouses, dormers, attics, gardens, rooftop parties

The lower third of Times New Roman holding up a poem whited-out
-in fog. Ivy covers fallen institutions, kudzu, edifices, employers

Meanwhile, down below, syllables
grow into houseplants.

The collector stores illustrations from dreams, cut-outs of conversation
high on a shelf in a hallway long and narrow as a sentence

- so it's like a room of stone creatures: marble rabbits, pheasants, lions,
stags, frogs, peacocks, horses, mice, hounds, an alligator, knick knacks

but also waylaid streets, blueprints for missed opportunities,

pale drawings of heavy items.
Maps to a kitchen of equilibrium.

The Old Show

These words are on timers, words with short life spans, color-coded words, aphid green, baby lotion pink, periwinkle—flash in __________ and out __________ on a midsummer night. The lifespan of these words is as brief as a minute or a day, as *mayflies, lightning bugs, damsel flies* in a wedding party of shooting stars, galaxy of moon calendars. Come and play, everything's A-Okay, neighbors there, that's where we meet. The words in the dark house flash in __________ and out __________. D^{22} D^{1} and F^{19} start to chase; the colors drag race, grabbing each other's long-tailed plumage of comet. This is when G^{29} appears. G^{29} could be translated as "One of these is not like the other." D^{81} can mean ____________________ while H^{5299} answers that all are on timers, flashing in and out of sight.

Luis instructs in his fix-it shop. Someone giggles over the letter K. *This is where milk comes from.* One of these is not like the other. Two plastic figures meet on top of a cake decorated with olive trees, join hands, dash down. The newborn is sleeping upstairs, swaddled in line breaks. Words on timers: Tang, cucumber sandwiches, jelly and cheese sandwiches, Miracle Whip, Hamburger Helper, Country-Time, liverwurst, Kool Whip, Rice a Roni, creamsicles, crunch sound of Big Wheels in the driveway.

Coda:
Words on timers,
Can you tell me how to get to, how to get to.
This is how your life goes.
In a different font, on timers of color,
flashing in and out of sight.

Gallery, Galaxy

The figures of allegory huddle on flotillas of agenda
        on their flotillas of agenda,

E-signed documents   held by angels
from the messenger service.

Europa, pale, big thighed,
                    accustomed to riding percheron of weather

balances on a PDF pontoon boat,
the Field Commander trans
                              forms into a dolphin.
The stern man in a moth-eaten crimson suit
                              on his cathedra carried onto a row boat,
entourage of naked and pained saints

                    in a sea of man-of-war, frigate, aircraft carriers
autocorrected to *flotillas of agenda*:

"All parties agree to set aside
their world-cracking differences"

                    & so the sky replaces the cathedral ceiling.

DECA-MERON

"How I make my way through this thicket of information—how I manage it, how I parse it, how I organize and distribute it." (Kenneth Goldsmith)

"Blessed citation! Among all the words in our vocabulary, it has the privilege of simultaneously representing two operations, one of removal, the other of graft, as well as the object of these operations—the object removed and the object grafted on, as if the word remained the same in these two different states." (Antoine Compagnon)

"Because I could not stop for Death—" (Emily Dickinson)

"Ever since the world began, men have been subject to the various tricks of Fortune, and it will ever be thus until the end." *Spray your Amazon packages.* Just leave it at the door. Thanks. These instructions were overheard from kitchens, basement apartments, half-opened garages, and second floor windows throughout the day, as could be heard floral and laurel laughter in the garden maze at any hour except siesta. The garden maze of shoulder-high hedges turned around the property; composed from sophisticated grafts, these [green sentences] made interchangeable fourteenth century Florence with twenty-first century northeastern United States, and constructed from a story-within-a-story, story ten times ten, for there were ten youths, seven women in their early twenties and three equally jejune men who had committed to each telling a tale to occupy their fourteen days safely together. *As in a waiting room on Zoom*, the seven maidens and three knaves sit on the lawn of the preface, the maidens plaiting wild flowers into each other's hair, worn loose **unbound** in the style of the age, or else gently debating the merits of taking the Pass/Fail option at the distant castles of universities, lute music playing on a soundbox™... *In the early spring of the year the plague began, in a terrifying and extraordinary manner, to make its disastrous effects apparent.* Numerous instructions were issued for safeguarding people's health, but to no avail. "How could that be?" The same was said in Florence and in an American city. Whatever its cause, the disease that had decimated their city had originated some months earlier in the East[1] where it had claimed countless lives before it "unhappily spread westward," growing in strength as it swept relentlessly on from one place to the next [2,13].

•

It was a time of tremendous sorrow. For not only did people die without having many family members or friends about them, but a great number departed this life without anyone at all to witness their going.[19] Online funeral services, held on Facebook or Zoom, people dressed in mourning and holding laptops. Here one day, gone the next, falling directly into the pit as "they extracted the bodies of the dead from their houses and left them lying outside their front doors, where anyone going about the streets, especially in the early morning, could have observed countless numbers of them." The horse of bones could be seen turning the corner to the Palazzo Vecchio, to the Bargello. [On one of the morgue trucks of the city] "a dying bouquet of flowers was strapped to the metal barrier that closes off the truck from the street, and on the side of the container were the faintly spray-painted words, 'Dead Inside.'" *NYT*, May 27, 2020. ( ). Oh, ( ). On Utica Avenue, *"Mr. Cleckley said he had used the trucks for overflow storage, but only after he had filled his chapel with more than 100 corpses. 'Bodies are coming out of our ears.'" (NYT, April 29, 2020).* People were dying in isolation in florescent hospital rooms, not enough ventilators, "the ones helping or burying the sick becoming themselves rapidly ill and dying," insufficient personal protection equipment. Such was the multitude of corpses (of which further consignments were arriving every day and almost by the hour at each of the churches), that there was not sufficient consecrated ground for them to be buried in...huge trenches were excavated in the churchyards, into which new arrivals were placed in their hundreds, stowed tier upon tier like ships' cargo, each layer of corpses being covered with a thin layer of soil till the trench was filled "to the top."

•

Those professions of close contact with the bodies of others were suspended, their practitioners left unsure about their livelihood, awaiting governmental edict. Still others were given status of essential and were asked to volunteer their health and possibly life to obey their employer and so prevent economic carnage. To support their families, youth the same age as our maidens and gentlemen in the Waiting Room in the garden of this narrative were hired at grocery stores and pharmacies or to deliver packages, masks hanging from van rear view mirrors. "Fewer and fewer people were coming to work—the person from the Meat Department didn't show up, then the Deli, then the Fish Counter—and so I was doing a lot of overtime. Was I worried? Yes, but what choice…" *Hence the countless numbers of people who fell ill were entirely dependent upon either the charity of friends or servants* and in performing this kind of service, those who served occasionally lost their lives as well as their earnings. "On Tuesday at work, she started coughing and had to turn away from the client's bed until told to go home." Their jobs became a source of horror. Still others' end of unemployment benefits became a cause of insomnia. For those who conducted business or lessons from home, it was customary portraiture to pose before (preferably white) bookshelves with curated objects, book titles, and photographs of nuclear family or of the powerful and famous, or to use a green screen, *i.e.*, a saint's lonely mountain & a winding road through cypress or the Virgin Mary were most popular. These people were not eager to return to commutes or office politics. *Working virtually will be the new normal. Office centricity is over. NYT,* June 29, 2020.

•

Some people were of the opinion that a sober and abstemious mode of living considerably reduced the risk of infection.[27, 6, 103, 56, 85, 92] Having withdrawn to their comfortable abode where there were no sick persons, they locked themselves in. Their salary (unfurloughed as of late spring) appearing automatically in their coffers. They refrained from speaking with outsiders, *refused to receive news of the dead or the sick*, and entertained themselves with whatever amusements they were able to devise, binge watching Netflix, wearing yoga pants: "It was merely a question of one citizen avoiding another, and of people almost invariably neglecting their neighbors and rarely or never visiting their relatives, addressing them only from a distance." Those related by blood, marriage, or romance stayed six feet away from other groups related by blood, marriage, or romance, selling cars, inspecting power lines, chatting with neighbors, celebrating Easter and Mother's Day on plastic benches set apart (excepting those attending rallies). This scene was repeated in meadows and lawns, on the pavement before big box stores and grocery stores. It replaced the previous universal symbol of humanity: a figure consulting a smart phone.

Others maintained that an infallible way of warding off this appalling evil was to enjoy life to the full through merrymaking, gratifying one's cravings whenever the opportunity offered, and shrugging the whole thing off as *uno scherzo enorme*. They flocked to beaches on the Eastern seaboard or tossed beads at carnivals in the South, stepping into vomit puddles dusted with sawdust. They visited one tavern after another, or they did their drinking "in various private houses, but only in ones where the conversation was restricted to subjects that were pleasant or entertaining." They held parties with prizes to the first to be infected. Still others organized caravans and encircled state capitols, honking horns.

Still others maintained that there was no better or more efficacious remedy against a plague than to run away from it. Swayed by this argument, and sparing no thought for anyone but themselves, large numbers of men and women abandoned their city, their homes, their relatives, their estates and their belongings, and headed for the country side, an uptick of direct flights to Florida, road trips to Vermont, rentals in the Catskills, Hamptons.

•

The more I reflect upon all this misery, the deeper my sense of personal sorrow; hence I shall refrain from describing those aspects which can suitably be omitted, and proceed to inform you that these were the conditions prevailing in our city, which was almost emptied of its inhabitants, its restaurants and businesses shuttered, its public transport systems carrying one or two masked, downcast riders, when one Tuesday morning, seven young women, fresh from college semesters that had ended at mid-point, wearing masks of richly patterned fabric, found themselves socially distancing on pews in the deserted Cathedral of Santa Maria Poema because "[t]he scene for the beginning of the frame story (in preference, say, to a more centrally located church such as the Florentine cathedral, or Duomo) was probably selected because of the association of its name with the telling of a story, or *novella*."

•

To idle the time, one young woman majoring in economics carried a copy of *The Grapes of Wrath* in her vegan leather messenger bag; two of the other young women carried copies of *Love in the Time of Cholera*, and Lauretta, the more charismatic of the group, *The Decameron* in her hobo bag, for it was she who first proposed that they leave the city together, borrowing the idea from the older author.

•

Lucas volunteered his family's second home. They could take three vehicles. Maria and Jose, the personal chef and the housekeeper of Giovanna's family, could be sent ahead to ready the house which had not been used since the previous summer. Giovanna's parents could spare them.

•

These lithe, fawn-like women in their early twenties were straight out of Botticelli, while the young men shared the long-locked looks of a young Michelangelo. If the Birth of Venus wore a N95 particulate mask, if the statue David wore a DIY mask, it would be these ten, without irony. While their friends watched *The Office* and wore sweats 24/7, they dressed elegantly and shaved or arranged their hair, fitting in a workout in Lucas' basement gym. They were "well mannered" with a quiet, partial awareness of their privilege which tempered their interactions with essential workers who serviced the house, to whom they repeated their gratitude, Thank you. Be safe. Just leave the package on the driveway. The plumber[9, 110] showed up on the fifth afternoon with his son, who had to withdraw from the state university where before the pandemic he could barely afford tuition. Leaf blowers and riding lawn mowers operated by townies made quick work of the acres every Thursday, hardly disturbing the pet stag & the peacocks.

The ten youth partook of delicacies and fine wines from their host's parents' wine cellar, for they were epicureans even at their modest ages, having been brought to Michelin star restaurants and to Italy and Provence as children. Though the land lay fallow, implements scattered on the ground where last used, but yet the delicacies still kept appearing, fruits and vegetables and organic snacks, mysteriously. If they ordered a shirt online from Aeropostale or a push-up bra at Victoria's Secret at drastic price reduction, it arrived, only a few days tardy, same for books or beauty products bought on Amazon, "the 'Clear Winner' from COVID-19 Lockdowns." By mid-April, it became clear that deliveries of the normal would not end, at least for now.

•

For the first few days, they kept the same schedule, not sure whether it was a Monday or Tuesday, Saturday or Sunday, with the custom of eating brunch in the courtyard, playing board games in their private quarters, reading, or watching YouTube videos. The ten youth gathered at noon after the delicacies were set out by Jose and Maria to watch the "plague diaries," daily briefings from their governor. Vaccine or no vaccine, when, tests or no tests. Injections of detergent. Taking a Clorox bath. Happy Science & "spiritual vaccines." A family pack of hydroxychloroquine and azithromycin, retailed at $3,995 for a family of four. Perhaps the nature of the illness was such that it allowed no remedy; or perhaps those people who were treating the illness, ignorant of its causes, were not prescribing the appropriate cure. And so the ten youth agreed that they would no longer turn on CNN at noon, or in their private quarters at lauds, matins, or vespers, for it was no longer tolerable to hear about swallowing detergents.

By the fourth day, Lucas thought it amusing to remove from the walls of his father's study a [plague mask] made in China bought on vacation in Venice, with its beak for vinegar, flowers or herbs. He donned the mask and paraded around his family's cinema, an antic which they found mildly distasteful but forbore, keeping in mind Lucas' loss, his grandfather, a survivor of horrors of the previous century, in a nursing home upstate. Nevertheless, it was clear to Lauretta that they needed to avoid sinking into *ribald despair* or callousness.

•

Blocking the movie screen onto which they had previously cast CNN, their wise queen announced, "Good friends, let us entertain ourselves differently, decrease screen time by telling stories, ten a day, one per person, on a theme." A leader was appointed for each day, and she or he decided the theme of the following day's stories, announced at the fire pit. What follows is a few days' worth of topics:

- Heroes and heroines without principles
- Heroes and heroines whose principles lead to temporary sorrows
- Hollywood romances and pregnancies
- Buckingham Palace scandal
- Tales of tremendous weight loss or gain
- Treacherous individuals in positions of trust or power

- Trustworthy individuals in treacherous situations without power
- Comeback stories after repentance

They remained regal in their propriety, faithful to relationships back in the city, although their daily tales were bawdy, the hijinks of Hollywood, politicians, religious leaders, massive cover ups, scandals, bed hopping, photo shopping, bribes.[112] They were removed from the troubles of the world, except for the fifth day at vespers when a tremendous row was heard from the summer kitchen. When the youth rushed to see if an accident had befallen the staff, they discovered Maria and Jose shouting in Spanish at the granite kitchen island. Jose had not washed his hands at the kitchen sink upon returning with grocery bags from Whole Foods, not singing even one round of *Happy Birthday*. It took much diplomacy for the youths to quiet Maria, who had lost several family members in the city to the disease, but they were unable to prevent Jose from quitting. He packed his belongings from the servant quarters, called a friend to pick him up, and departed within the hour. The ten youth conferred and agreed that this crisis could be addressed. Two of the young women had sufficient kitchen skills to help out, having taken private lessons with a TV chef in boarding school, though who was to fetch groceries was still undetermined by the evening, until Maria made a few phone calls and hired a youth from town.

•

Gathering around the fire pit, watching the heaped-up sunset, pulling on ivy league sweatshirts to ward off the chill, they wondered what was happening outside the gates of their host's property, the suffering and job loss, dreams and expectations assassinated from one month to the next, from middle class to a bread line in thirty days, supply lines and fields unpicked, unplanted.

•

One evening after the next day's theme had been announced, Phillipa said to the agreement of the others, "It will be six days since we came to stay here, and to avoid being joined by others, I think it is advisable for us to move elsewhere. I have already thought of a place for us to go, and made the necessary arrangements." [28a, 89]

•

They caravanned to Marco's family's Italianate villa, which had the elaborate gardens necessary to this borrowed tale and a central courtyard that stayed cool during the noon hour. But their friends in the city were regularly texting them, and their isolation might soon be broken. Furthermore, they were concerned about decorum. Although they were unaffected by the stories they told one another, behaving like siblings and communicating regularly to their significant others living afar, people talk. Also an apex seemed to be reached in the city. A day with 248 deaths in their state was viewed as an improvement though it seemed a famine might set in, the jobs report grim, the worst unemployment rate, 14.7%, since the Great Depression.

•

And so it was that after the tenth story on the tenth day, they agreed to end their self-quarantine, though fourteen days was recommended, not ten. They would continue to quarantine at home with their families. Next morning they arose at the crack of dawn, their trunks, suitcases, and duffel bags sent on ahead by the steward, and with their wise queen Lauretta leading the way, they drove into the city. The seven young women were dropped off outside Santa Maria Poema, no convenient parking spot found by their knaves, and each dispersed safely to their homes. The next few months would resemble the summers of high school, for internships at the law firm, non-profit, and art gallery were no longer feasible. *Thus until the end, and it will ever be, the various tricks of Fortune, men have been subject to. Ever since the world began.* Unexpectedly living at home again, they spent a lot of time in their air conditioned bedrooms, beckoned out to join family activities, spending more hours than ever with their parents and siblings, who were unaffected.

Passages in this intertextual garden were taken directly from Giovanni Boccaccio's The Decameron, *translated by G.H. McWilliam. Not all are demarcated; some are left unpruned and form a different maze of days.*

Alexandria Peary serves as New Hampshire Poet Laureate. The author of eight other books, her work has received an Academy of American Poets Laureate Fellowship, the Iowa Poetry Prize, the Slope Editions Book Prize, the Joseph Langland Prize, Best of New Hampshire, and three Best of the Net nominations. She specializes in mindful writing.

www.ingramcontent.com/pod-product-compliance
Lightning Source LLC
Chambersburg PA
CBHW011406070526
44577CB00003B/397
9781956005363